What I Meant To Say

By

Crystal Moungle

ISBN: 978-0-5783-8079-7

Acknowledgments

Wow, book number two is officially making its debut into the world! So happy that God chose me to become a writer and poet. I can't wait to keep flourishing and fulfilling God's plan. I want to send a huge thanks to my family, best friend, fiancé, and everyone else that supported me on my journey

Contents

What I meant to Say

I don't think you heard me the first time

That's why I came back

To remind you

What I meant to say is to pay attention

Keep your eyes on me

What's to follow is more

More of what I failed to say verbally but wrote

More lines that you can quote

What I meant to say is I'm not finished

CHAPTER 1

Self-Love /Care

"Love yourself first and everything else falls into line. You really have to love yourself to get anything done in this world."

— **Lucille Ball**

They call her beauty

Dear beautiful girl with the dimples on your legs
And rolls on your side
Tiger stripes line your hips and thighs
A scar above the bikini line to signify you've given life
Breast that use to sit high
Hair that used to embellish young age, with no grays
Your hair doesn't have to be done to know you're a masterpiece
Beauty is her name

Hershey's Skin Kisses

My skin tells the story of pressure made to build diamonds

A twisted, long, historical story that led to what's before your eyes

Skin as brown as an oak trunk, but I'm not planted in the ground

My skin reflects as part of the outline to the sky

Free, Smooth, and Clear

Unchained

Brown skin girl, nothing is the same

good Night

What's a woman to do
Saturday night, spent alone
But not in a bad way
Like it can sometimes feel
When my bank account is low and there are too many days before
payday
Or those nights where darkness follows and depression, exe's, and
random regrets creep in
No this is a night of relaxation
There is something in my cup, but it's more than that
At peace with where I am and where I know, I'm going
Times aren't like this always but somehow I always find my way
back
To this good night, good vibes,
The scales are no longer unbalanced and have found equilibrium
from within
All that matters is this moment where I can relish doing nothing at
all

Bare

You gone get tired of hiding your gold
Dimming your light so those around you can glow
Showing cubic zirconia, when really, you're a diamond
No synthesizing here, show it all
Down to your naked, bare draws

Greedy when it comes to me

Remove all the things you think make you, you
Peel back that potato skin and get to the root of you
So many things distract, meant to awaken the worldly thoughts
But not the Godly ones

Things like empathy, kindness, and forgiveness aren't priorities in
this world order
Greed and wealth encompass my thoughts more often than not
Wanting more never settling for less
Not realizing the real settle, is one of never being satisfied
A being that's never quite full, always hungry yearning for more

You could place me near the sea, and I'd still end up thirsty
Thirsty for the best version of me
Not the least

CHAPTER 2

Mental Health

"One small crack does not mean that you are broken, it means that you were put to the test, and you didn't fall apart."

— Linda Poindexter

Psyche

Mental health feels like taking time for me

Self-love on a Saturday, where the only intentions I care about are my own

I used to sit on the couch and tell a therapist my problems, and that worked

For a while

Mental health looks like me blowing up at you over small things, and then apologizing

It's not saying anything for over 24 hours to anyone

Focused on crawling out of my own mind

Realizing my triggers and need to avoid

Unloading all my thoughts wherever I can write

Therapy

I stopped going to therapy because I went for one problem and left with many

Realizing everything is connected to my behavior now

Change required much more than sitting on a couch once a week

A timeline of solving my problems and moving onto whatever else was next in my life

I thought it would be simple, but complexity and abstract is what I got

Behavior rooted in childhood tendencies, fear of my relationship being copy + paste of my family history

Challenges of someone else's failures leaking into my brain

The overachiever, problem-solver mentality

It's all linked to my reality

Anxious

Anxiety feels like crowded rooms and loud extroverts
Insecurity in the presence of perfection
Overthinking
Over analyzing
And over it

All at the same time

It's my mind hyping me up, and my body pushing me back down
Fast heartbeat, sweaty palms, and empty lies my mind tells

Stormy Weather

Depression feels like a hole you know you can crawl out of but can't seem to grasp the walls of

I can see that the skies are blue when I stare up above

It's knowing I'll get back to feeling hopeful, eventually

But knowing now is not the time or the day

A time to mull over my loneliness and doubts

My own personal black cloud, following me

But soon, the sun will shine

This is what I remember when I see an endless view of storm clouds hovering over me

Busy Bee

Why is it so hard to go easy on myself?
Even though I'm soft towards others
Struggling with showing myself there's time to unwind
Every day doesn't have to be jam-packed with stuff to do
Squeezing a size 10 into a size 7 shoe
That's how tight my days have been
I gotta slow down
That's what I tell myself
But I have to get stuff done

Undiagnosed

I'm starting to think we're all just a little mentally ill

Swallow this pill

One in the morning, and one before bed

Staying medicated just to avoid this feeling of dread or sometimes to ease the mind

Weed, that's a stimulant

Alcohol makes me forget

Are we all undiagnosed because we avoid going to the doctor

Shit, I don't want to find out I have a problem
One that can't be cured or saved with some simple prescription

Stressing about things you can't control; your blood pressure is sky high

And even with this advice from the listening ear, you choose not to listen

Is this worry or obsession with trying to correct your wrongs

Fear of being diagnosed

CHAPTER 3

F*** Boys

"A bad relationship can do that; can make you doubt everything good you ever felt about yourself."

— Dionne Warwick

Nobody's Victim

Navigating a world where being too sexy feels like it can lead to being victimized

I can only look nice sometimes

Aggression can be attractive, but it can also be disturbing to a high degree

I can only look nice sometimes

I throw on my sweats and a hoodie when I step out after dark, not even that halts this feeling of being watched

I want to be seen, but not to the degree

Of feeling stalked, harassed, and beaten

Not making contact, or being ingenuine to the smile that usually rests on my face

All so I can only look nice sometimes

Fear of being grateful that I've never been violated, but knowing age is nothing to these strangers that fill the streets

It's not safe for women, whether we're dressed down or ready to paint the town

No receipt

No transaction available to reference all the time wasted

No receipt

For the times I took care of you whether it was making love even when I wanted to lay there

Or displaying feign interest

Where is my return on my claim?

Can I get a refund for my kisses, make a return on these not-good-enough feelings?

There's no exchange

There's no way a rebate would gratify this stupidity

I needed retribution when I was unhappy but instead, I stayed

Fuck your receipt all I want is an acknowledgement that this was a disclosed sale

I want my time and wasted effort back

The problem is I don't have a receipt for all the shit I endured for you

And now I don't even have that

Wasteland

Are you actually telling me some men didn't plan to not be
fathers?
Even after they released seeds inside a womb
You weren't ready for a kid, but you were ready to make love
As He/She grew inside of me you abandoned me and everything
we said we would do
Your lack of actions were tolerated when it was just us
But they became unacceptable once there was a result of our lust
You claim to love this little one that will soon take a path similar to
you and me
Yet when it comes to evoking change, this path is one you can't see
Blinded by other women, friends, and life
Your problem is you think you have time
All the time in the world to show up, be second-best parent
Where would our union of love be if it weren't for me
Bending, breaking, then forming again
Holding it all together, for the children
I know this isn't the measure of a love you promised was endless, a
love that would extend to our child
But I've lied to myself more than once when it comes to you
So why would the present be any different
You're still full of shit and empty promises, pinky swear, I want to
do what's right

But you still get shit wrong
You force me to explain your absence and wipe the tears away
Theirs and my own
I thought you were different, even if you weren't with me
But it's clear it means nothing since you abandoned your seed

Get yo Shit (Angela basset voice)

Funny how it felt like it took me forever to get over you

Get yo shit I don't just mean that little box of stuff

Get your insecurities that you reflected onto me

Get your image of a woman being her all and you providing less

Calling me for simple shit

Access denied

You can no longer have me
Leave those problems for the next woman, your issues are just that

Yours

Get yo shit, and don't turn back

There's nothing more left for you to access

The hold you use to have on me has disappeared

Guess it went missing around the same time I stopped letting you inside of me

Not just physically

In every way, I have separated myself from you

Get yo shit, and don't look back

Source Waiting to Exhale"

The Noise

Something about her screams and her baby's cries don't sit right with me

It doesn't happen all the time, just occasionally

I feel powerless because I don't know her

I just see her in passing

I don't want to get involved but something about this feels off

I fear for her life and wonder why she allows him to keep coming back

Replaying this scene

He continues to scream, I know if I heard it, then so did all my other neighbors

Yet we all stay in our respective space

Is this cowardice or safety?

There's no telling what could happen

All I know is this pain of hearing someone as delicate as you, a woman

Isn't meant for my ears

Harder

It's already hard enough to be this person you see
I hold my head up high because I can't stand to see it down
These things you place on me, you can't even fathom for yourself
Like if I asked the same of you, your palm would be outstretched
for help
Perfection you chase within me but refuse to look at your own
scars
I thought we were building up, making a foundation
But just like cookies crumble so did we
And even though you're gone, pieces of what you said still ring in
my ears
Your name, your thoughts, tatted on my body, memories of you
Things I can never forget but I'm trying, just like I scrub away all
the shit from previous days
I know that sometime soon I'll be rid of you, all the bullshit you
put us through
Shit is already hard enough, but you just had to make it harder
And unlike the past, I welcome this new chapter

CHAPTER 4

Sweetheart

"You know you're in love when you can't fall asleep because reality is finally better than your dreams."

— Dr. Seuss

Don't Wake Me

I keep asking myself when I'll wake up from this dream of you
The truth is I don't want to
There will never be enough pinches to my cheek to wake me from
this dream
I keep thinking when will madness and chaos erupt
But it's withdrawn into you
Sometimes I see that fire building in your eyes and the smoke
coming from your ears
But you let it dissipate
Just like everything else in this dream I don't know how or when I
got here
Just know it's currently where I'm at
I keep thinking why me?
Or why you?
The truth of the matter, it's not for me to understand
All I know is I'm stuck in the REM stage, and I can't decipher
fiction from life
But I'll stay here with you in my consciousness
Dreamland
Where perfection is endless, and mistakes don't exist
When will I wake up from this dream of you that persists?

Treasure Chest

I could've sworn Midas touched you because you are golden

You shine, baby you shine

If no one was looking I'd still have my eye on you

I know I don't say if often, and express my appreciation in ways that may be silent to you

Blame it on our love languages

With all things uncertain, I know for sure

You are golden

Profusely

My heart was profusely beating
My love was forever leaving
A ghost from the past reared its ugly head
Prayer kept me leveled
Memories fade yet reappear
Emotions, feelings all so dear
When it comes to you my heart speeds up
No slowing down

For Me

You're for me, not for everybody
I love it when I don't have to second guess your loyalty
It's very clear you stand with me, and I stand by you
We have a chemistry that can't be defined by just some four-letter
word
Our bond is deeper than Atlantis and higher than Mount Everest
Not to make things one-sided I just want to show my appreciation
The care you show me when I'm at my best and at my worst
When I need a reassuring voice, and someone to triumph with

Something about you is for me

CHAPTER 5

Black America

Injustice anywhere is a threat to justice everywhere.

— **Martin Luther King, Jr.**

You're not to be so blind with patriotism that you can't face reality. Wrong is wrong, no matter who does it or says it.

— **Malcolm X**

Corporate

When I wake up in the morning, I paint my face
Not with that stuff from Home Depot or Lowe's

I tie up pieces of the real me in my shoelaces and pull the less
intimidating side out through my lips
I brush my tongue so I can get all the street colloquial language I
know to be me, scrubbed clean

I tune my voice box even better than autotune, so there's no hint
of any forwardness and threat

I choose my attire carefully; it doesn't take much for my roots to
show
My chest is expansive without even trying
The curve of my backside can't be contained

Following policy, I say to myself

Yes, I keep my hair done
No, you can't touch my hair

Shameless gentrification

No piece of the land untouched

The same thing that makes this home is the same thing that keeps changing

The street geologically is the same, but it looks different
When I had a dime to my name, I could've bought a piece of my childhood

And now that I've got a few dollars it's damn near impossible to think of owning

Something worth living in on the street of my childhood

Knee scrapes, streetlights, memories you can't just forget about

Memories of a less safe community, one where you couldn't be in the streets, past curfew at least from my perspective and that of the local news

What's changed

Is it the fact that other types of people moved in

Taxes skyrocketed and income stayed the same for those with more
knowledge of this community more than just knowing a street
name

All over America, we assign this type of feeling a name

Gentrification

What about black trauma?

My palm is outstretched, and my temples are tense

This is that same feeling I get

When the world looks on at us, the black community gauging our reaction to the series of tragedies that have become someone's life

Usually ending up in settlements or injustice, you choose

Instead of us, it's a different set of human beings whose value has just been reduced

WW3 is what people are calling it, do you know what happened the last time there was widespread war

Do you know what will happen this time, will we finally become extinct like the dinosaurs?

I have all these feelings and thoughts in my medulla, but I still, have hope
I still try today because I still see the future in my reach

But I'm not saying it's easy

When I see funds so easily released, but when I was in a financial bind there was no sight of any money trees

I don't want to compare trauma because that's unfair, but there's something unsettling knowing my own country doesn't show me the same care

Outspoken

Sometimes I try to live like MLK back in his early nonviolent days

Stating his opinion but avoiding conflict

But after I've had enough, I turn into the opposition

Detroit Red, El Shabazz

You know his name, the man that you could hear a mile away

Not afraid to lift every voice, fist, and gun

There comes a time when being soft-spoken just won't work

Because certain words need to be said and heard clearly

There's no repeating what's about to come next

I must get this off my chest

Because to some silence can be seen as weakness and an invitation
to step on and over me
Outspoken because I must be

40 acres and a mule

I have ancestors that left me something

I'm not talking hundreds of years ago, I'm talking a few decades

A lineage that I don't know but can see in a photo album

They left a little piece of themselves, speaking to the hardship and strength to own

They worked the land, hell even picked cotton

Just for their piece of American pie, but really it could be equivalent to a crumb

Leftovers, Scraps

That's nothing new

A stretch of land situated in the part of town only Black people were supposed to live

A few decades ago, now it's turned into an area of revitalization, renewal, and growth

Fancy words to tell me that there's another purpose wanted for this community

I have ancestors that left something within me

African American

People speak of feeling split between two worlds

One where they must adjust to life here and still carry their traditions and culture from the place where they originated

They can speak their native tongue, and carry out practices of religion

But when I look in the mirror the crack of splitting worlds is harder to decipher

I have no native tongue it was outlawed
I have no native home because it was taken
I have a religion I believe in but unsure if my ancestors practiced the same

I've never visited the motherland but have heard tales of people like me still being looked at funny

Not just because they're American but because they are black

The people we're supposed to identify with don't want to be associated with us

CHAPTER 6

Writer's Block

"I have fallen in love with the imagination. And if you fall in love with the imagination, you understand that it is a free spirit. It will go anywhere and it can do anything."

— Alice Walker

All Mines

Intellectual property, have to keep my ideas protected
Not for lack of sharing
But to protect myself
In a world where we're all a bunch of copycats
Myself included
Sometimes it's hard to even come up with an original thought
There's a wealth of knowledge buried within me that keeps
pushing up every so often
What would I look like, giving away my treasures so easily
To be taken advantage of, not by anyone
My defenses are up because they must be
I'm tired of hearing stories about people with talent being shorted
Shorted out of a vision that was theirs to begin with
There is no dollar sign on my soul, nor will there be one on my
talent, both are limitless
I have something you can't buy or steal
It's a secret all my own
The truth is you have something buried inside you too
But this here is mine, you've got to discover your own worth

The Process

Another sleepless night, up thinking about nothing
My eyes are heavy but apparently, my subconscious is heavier
Staring into an empty room, nothing but my apartment landscape
smiling back at me
I find myself someplace else, somewhere familiar, like home
Typing away this poem
4 o clock in the morning sounds about right for me, the time when
my brain comes to light
Waking the rest of me, maybe after this, I can go back to sleep
Word vomit escapes in one of the places that feel like home for
bare mineral thoughts
Thinking of everything, and nothing in the same breath
My curtains are closing on my eyelids, guess that means I'm done

Like Water

Having a gift is like a deep well, in which discovery and adventure is required

Knowing your gift is the knowledge that the well is endless and abundant

Turning off this faucet isn't possible when it comes to what I write

Sometimes the pressure is slow and steady

Other times the words come spilling out my spout

Too fast to remember and too quick to let go

My piece of the Pie

On the cusp of transforming
From feeling like that girl to that woman
Will this next level come like I know it will
Will I, the latecomer
Be ahead of the curve to prove something I believed long ago
That I am that girl
That force
That light
Or will I just become a distant memory of my dreams?
Fantasizing daydreaming of leveling up
But really leveling down is a possibility too
Thinking of that what if's or more like whatnot
If I follow this path what could lie behind
A wall of regret for sharing something so precious as my thoughts
To a bunch of strangers
But wouldn't it be worth it to make at least one person feel
To know that someone as hopeful but flawed as them can say
they'll do something and never give up
I don't know how I'll get to my personal wealth of jewels promised
to me
But all I know is since I've started this journey
Things weigh less, and sometimes I get the crazy eye

For dreaming so big and wide, but to those that love me they still tell me to reach for the sky

Multitasking

Making time for what I love while also punching that clock
After this 9-5 it's nonstop
My eyes are tired, but my heart feels good
Trying to see one streamed income in my rearview and mogul in
my passenger seat
So many ideas in my iPhone notes, but no idea how to make this
shit real
But it's ok I don't have to know
This is a path where I just do and carry faith

CHAPTER 7

What is Meant to Come

"The future depends on what we do in the present."

— Mahatma Gandhi

Planted Seeds

Wishing upon a star for you to come my way
You were mine before we ever met
And made for me before ever being conceived

I'm praying for my health, for my body, and the strength to be your
mom
Praying your dad and I can make it so you'll have us both through
a lifetime

I can't wait to see that twinkle in your eyes and watch how you
grow,

But what I don't mind waiting for, is staying up with you in the
wee mornings of the hour, constant baby shows, and changing
body parts

For better or for Worse
I am yours and you are mine

At the age where women get worried about not being barren
Seeing all my classmates and friends
Start a journey I haven't yet began

Wondering if my bodies good enough to hold someone else
Long enough for nine months
Sometimes I barely have my own shit together
But I'd act like skies are always blue, and the sun was high in the sky for

Three
Six
Five

Just to meet you

Up Next

I keep my old pics up just so you can see the glow up
Never been picture perfect
But even time can't deny, it's my time up
Waited enough for things to go my way, guess I gotta make my
own fate
My mind is made, there won't be any turning back
This time I'm detached
Bungee cord, the parachute opens

Blessing, on blessings

Lately what I've been manifesting is coming to fruition
I've been in my bag, but I've also been in my word and my prayers
Blessings on blessings are what I'm after
Speaking good into existence, flooding out the bad
I don't light sage, but those bad spirits finally feel like they're off
me
Completely, no coming back
Bon voyage to that
With all these blessings stacking up
It's time to share the overflow

Making Moves

Where you pause is not where you finish
Destiny awaits, there's still time to change your fate
Where you are presently has nothing to do with your ending

With all the garbage from your past, there won't be a bag in sight
Your future is high, and the past is beneath you
Jealousy used to be your friend and misery was plenty of company

But that was when you thought your presence was the present
Looking beyond what you see has always been a challenge
But you are willing to overcome this hurdle to make it where you
need to go

The true gift is the knowledge you gain on this trip

Grace

Look at where you brought me from

Easy days don't come seldom

Yet here I am

Heartaches use to feel plentiful, but God here I am

Sex is still sinful, but here I am

Empty promises escape my mouth but still, here I am

Your ears, my prayers could have been null and void

But here I am

CHAPTER 8

Summer

"When the sun is shining, I can do anything; no mountain is too high, no trouble is too difficult to overcome."

— Wilma Rudolph

Family Reunion

I can see it all so clearly now

You + Me

Playing in the grass, getting our clothes stained

Picnic tables, and concrete sidewalks

An aroma of smells from hot dogs and hamburgers

To hot fried fish, only for adults they said

Drinks with the foil tops, that our little hands just couldn't seem to grasp

Loud, boisterous laughter at the card table, and a game of horseshoe's is what I see

A union of all these brown faces united by one single tethering string

The family tree

August Nights

I want every night to feel like summer
Not the temperature but the feeling
Thinking back to how I would stay up late nights when school was
out
There was no thinking about the next day only the night
Waking up on the regular at 2 in the afternoon
Sense of time, timeless

I miss that feeling of knowing each day would be the same
In a way that's nostalgic

Sun Kissed

Later for pumpkin spiced lattes

Now for ice cream melting down my hands

Tube tops, and shorts

Hot leather seats, crisp to my skin

Perspiration pooling under my breasts

Dark skin because of the sun

Cool summer nights when we sit on the porch

Mid-day muggy rain, that makes my hair thick

Fresh air, blooming flowers, and noise outside

Sunlight hitting my face, just right

Summer Baby

The sand beneath my toes tells me I've made it

Greeted with the warmth of the sun on a hot summer day
Wiggling my toes, a fresh pedicure merges with grains of graham
crackers

My eyes are drawn to the only thing that matters at this moment,
water
I use it to hydrate
I use it to refresh my body
But at this moment I want to be consumed by it

An ocean away is the normal theme of life and time
But when I stare at this endless blue, I forget it all

Author Bio

Crystal Moungle is a poet, writer, and book enthusiast. Born and raised in Charlotte, NC. She started writing poetry in middle school and throughout her college years. In addition to being a poet, she is passionate about financial literacy, traveling, and her family.

If you enjoyed this book, check out "Speak Up" the first series of poems published by Crystal.

Did you love What I Meant to Say?
Scan the code below to check out other upcoming releases from Crystal and events happening near you.

www.ingramcontent.com/pod-product-compliance
Lightning Source LLC
Chambersburg PA
CBHW060201070426
42447CB00033B/2250